DEEP CONVERSATIONS
with the
HOLY SPIRIT

Key Words Version

EMMANUEL ETIM

For more information and
Special offers from Emmanuel Etim library, email us at
library@apostleemmanuel.org

Deep Conversations with the Holy Spirit

Deep Conversations with the Holy Spirit

Unless otherwise indicated, all Scripture references are taken from the new King James Version, © 1979, 1980, 1982, 1984, by Thomas Nelson, Inc. Used by permission. All rights reserved.

DEEP CONVERSATIONS WITH THE HOLY SPIRIT
Key Words version, is published by AEEM Publishing
ISBN: 978-0-9997241-6-3
First Print © 2013; Second print © 2014
By Emmanuel Etim

The rights of Apostle Emmanuel Ishie Etim to be identified as he reserves the authorship of this work in accordance with International copyright laws:

Written permission must be secured from the author to use or reproduce any part of this book, except for brief quotations in critical reviews or articles, with appropriate reference suggested style Etim E, (2013) 'Deep Conversations with the Holy Spirit' Key Words version AEEM Publishing

Cover design: Wilcox Onyemekeihia

For more information about the Ministry activities, speaking appointments and travel schedule of Apostle Emmanuel Ishie Etim, contact the address below:

P. O. Box 50203
Ikoyi, 101008
LAGOS STATE
NIGERIA
Tel: Nigeria +2349052280561; Ethiopia +251911686246
Email: president@apostleemmanuel.org
Website: http://www.apostleemmanuel.org

INTRODUCTION

When you study these conversations, give yourself diligently to them through contemplation and meditation, because they are not brought to you based on self-opinion. My friend Rev Julian Kyula, inspired by the Holy Spirit, declares self-opinion to be the weakest form of intelligence and deduction.

This book, is also not written to be a theoretical rendition of canon writings: It is beyond hypothetical observation of occurrence and/or the systematic presentation of written scripture.

It is a book of spoken words by the Spirit: the power of scripture encapsulated. Not as an orator, or of a good speaker, effective communicator or motivation; but they are Words! Words! Words! Wow: Harvested from experiential interaction in the realm of the spirit as secrets to the universalism of what Jesus said in John 6:63, *"The words I speak unto you are spirit and life".*

I bring it to you, confident in its dynamic power, enabled to cause activation in the influence of the Spirit inside out, to such a degree, you will experience a cognitive dissonance.

It is for everyone: Ministers, Pastors, Church workers, new converts, old and young, men and women, all nationalities. It can be used as a devotional and journal, as a reference and guide for sermons, evangelism, counseling, cell group meetings, bible study, and more.

Be a blessing as you drink of this divine water.

- Apostle Emmanuel Etim

ACKNOWLDGEMENT

This work would not have been so smooth from start to finish, without the excitement, commitment and investment of pastor Eromosele. A diligent student of the bible: he put in hours, weeks, and years into this work as a scribe. Thank you and God bless you.

I also appreciate immensely the support given to him by Getenet Lakew, a young man; rich in knowledge and grace: such a one given to me exceptionally for the work in East Africa and who graciously helped with the Amharic version (Ethiopian dialect).

Yonas Bekele as we revised it together and extracting the beauty of fellowship and passion he has for the understanding of every message expressed in this book. God bless you all and your labor of love will bear generational fruits.

When you experience that, answers (response) to your prayers are guaranteed, the how and what you pray for will change.

FURTHER READING
1JOHN 5:14-15;
MATTHEW 20:20;
MARK 10:35.

Man, don't marry a religious lady: find a God fearing woman.

FURTHER STUDY
PROVERB 31:10-31

If you knew, what is in the future 10 years ahead, what would you do differently today?

FURTHER STUDY
HEBREW 12:2;
JEREMIAH 29:11;
1 CORINTHIANS 9:26-27

Woman, don't marry a God fearing man but seek after a man that loves God.

**FURTHER STUDY
EPHESIANS 5:25-28;
2 CORINTHIANS 5:14;
JOHN 14:15, 10:27**

*Men, do not marry a woman;
marry a wife.*

<u>FURTHER STUDY</u>
PROVERB 18:22

You have heard before: As you think, so you are, but now i say to you, what you say you become.

**FURTHER STUDY
ROMANS 10:9-10;
MATTHEW 12:37;
JOEL 3:10;
JOSHUA 1:8;
PSALM 1:2**

Half obedience is the same as no obedience at all.

FURTHER STUDY
2-1SAMUEL 15:23;
JAMES 2:10;
NUMBERS 33:50-56

If you are not in a position to receive and manage responsibility with excellence, perseverance and diligence: you are a 'Nepios' (Grk-Childish).

FURTHER STUDY

GALATIANS 4:1-2;

1 CORINTHIANS 13: 11

You have heard before: the fear of God births wisdom; now I also say to you, to love is wisdom.

FURTHER STUDY
PROVERBS 4:7;
1 CORINTHIANS 13:13;
JOHN 13:34

When you recognize the seemingly little moves of God, you are ready to operate-in and receive the mighty works.

FURTHER STUDY
PROVERBS 31:10-31

Walking with God will result in a life of distinction, excellence and extraordinary 'everything'.

**FURTHER STUDY
GENESIS 5:24;
DANIEL 1:19-20; 5:12; 6:3;
PSALM 37:23;
GALATIANS 5:16, 5:25**

As child of God, the more it appears you are being suppressed; the higher you go.

FURTHER STUDY
2 CORINTHIANS 4:17

The longer you insist to be where God instructs otherwise; everything, as you knew it and know it, starts falling apart.

FURTHER STUDY
JONAH 1:10-11

You cannot be a failure, in anything you do, as long as you submit to the leading of the Holy Spirit. <u>Do it again and persevere.</u>

FURTHER STUDY
JAMES 1:25;
LUKE 5:1-6(5);
GALATIANS 6:9

The full assurance that you will accomplish your purpose in Christ; begins with selflessness, compassion and making no provision for the flesh.

FURTHER STUDY
EPHESIANS 5:25;
PHILIPPIANS 1:22-26;
2 TIMOTHY 4:7

The best place to be loyal is in the house of God; this is truth.

**FURTHER STUDY
GENESIS 49:26;
EXODUS 17:11;
LUKE 1:8 (5-14)**

A person who is always preoccupied with only daily human quest is outside of God's will.

FURTHER STUDY
MATTHEW 6:24-33;
ROMANS 8:5-8;
JAMES 4:3

Many Christians are still looking for Jesus today: we are not empowered to be disciples and followers of Jesus Christ but witnesses and saints.

FURTHER STUDY
ACT 1:8;
MATTHEW 5:13-14;
1 JOHN 4:17;
LUKE 10:19

A blessed man does not operate with the same rules of engagement, methods or styles as others.

FURTHER STUDY
2 CHRONICLE 20:15-26;
JOS 6:1-27;
2 KING 1-6;
1 SAMUEL 17:45-46;
COL 2:8:20-22

Your expectations in God are directly proportional to your experiences of God's manifested power.

**FURTHER STUDY
EPHESIANS 3:17-20;
HEBREW 6:1-2;
MATTHEW 9:18-2**

Did you know that God will not and cannot do anything on earth without a human ally? Become one today through partnership in giving.

FURTHER STUDY
PSALM 115:16

Please take this seriously: Observing spiritual instruction requires exercise, perseverance and worthy of the fight. It is not automatic.

FURTHER STUDY
ROMANS 13:14;
GALATIANS 5:16;
1 TIMOTHY 6:12, 4:7-8

Did you know, there are heights in God you won't be able to realize, if you neglect corporate fellowship: i.e attending church?

FURTHER STUDY
PSALM 73:17 (1-28);
LUKE 4:16;
ACTS 17:2;
HEBREW 10:25

If you must experience living above all kinds of powers;

Then you must walk always in the Spirit.

**FURTHER STUDY
2 PETER 1:4;
EPHESIANS 1:21, 2:6;
GALATIANS 5:25**

If you want to walk in the victory we already have in Christ Jesus, worship God in Spirit and Truth.

FURTHER STUDY
1 CORINTHIANS 15:57;
1 JOHN 5:4;
JOSHUA 6:1-27;
2 CHRONICLES 20:21-26;
EXODUS 15:11

> *To operate in the anointing, you need active and consistent fellowship with the Spirit.*

FURTHER STUDY
EPHESIANS 5:18-19;
JUDE 1:20;
1 TIMOTHY 4:14

Faithfulness in the days of obscurity is the ticket for your promotion.

FURTHER STUDY
GENESIS 39:7-10, 40:12-14, 41:11-15

The evidence of your spiritual maturity is in how far your words can reach.

**FURTHER STUDY
MATTHEW 4:4;
JOB 38:11;
LUKE 17:6;
ACT 13:6-11**

Don't be ignorant or naive: blood and logos {sciences, gnosticism and mythologies) can alter hierarchies in the spirit realm. Hitherto and forever, the blood of Jesus is the perfect and complete sacrifice.

**FURTHER STUDY
2 KINGS 3:25-27;
HEBREW 12:24;
EXODUS 7:11;
MATTHEW 2:2**

> *People are seldom worried by what they are going through, but more by what they can or cannot see ahead (certain of).*

FURTHER STUDY
2 Co 4:18;
HEBREW 12:2

You are fully spirit as you are flesh and blood. But the former needs more attention than the later.

FURTHER STUDY
1 PETER 1: 23;
JOHN 3:6;
GALATIANS 5: 16 & 18

The combination of Consistency, Continuity and Diligence are the secrets to good success.

**FURTHER STUDY
JAMES 2:25;
JOSHUA 1:8;
GALATIANS 6:9;
PROVERB 22:29**

As Christians, we are born into 'another realm'.

**FURTHER STUDY
2 PETER 1:4;
EPHESIANS 2:6**

The correct and present tense understanding in worship and praise produces confidence, boldness and propels you into prophetic utterances of spiritual authority.

**FURTHER STUDY
1 JOHN 4: 4,17;
1 JOHN 5:14-15;
PHILIPPIANS 1:6;
HEBREW 4:16;**

Seeking first the kingdom of God does not mean you are negligent of your essential needs and wants; it actually means, you have discovered the peaceful, safe, free, guaranteed and sustainable way to receive them.

FURTHER STUDY
LUKE 12:30;
MATTHEW 6:33

The fullness of the Holy Spirit activates the working of the word in you. This produces supernatural abilities and an irresistible aura in your life.

FURTHER STUDY
ACTS 5:15; 8:39-40; 28:3-6;
MARK 6:2;
MATTHEW 8:27

These five things independently or can combine to determine dreams:

What you hear or listen to; where and how you spend your time; what occupies your thought; what you say or confess; and whom you allow to influence you.

**FURTHER STUDY
PHILIPPIANS 3:17;
ECCLESIASTES 5:3;
MARK 11: 23-24;
MATTHEW 16:12**

When you disobey or ignore the Holy Spirit, you permit unpleasant situations and circumstances to hold you captive.

FURTHER STUDY
GALATIANS 5:17-18;
ACTS 27:10-12 & 21-25

The state of your spirit critically shapes your interaction and responses in the dream realm.

FURTHER STUDY
1 TIMOTHY 1:17;
LUKE 10:19;
MARK 16:18;
ROMANS 8:16

The greatest limitation the devil has influenced on earth is the question how?

**FURTHER STUDY
2 KINGS 7:1-2;
JUDGES 6:12-13;
LUKE 1:31,34**

Grow to the place where people, natural knowledge and sensory perceptions no longer influence you, but every spoken word of God.

**FURTHER STUDY
MATTHEW 4:4;
HEBREW 5:13-14;
EPHESIANS 4:14**

It is a lie from Satan that what you don't know cannot affect you: understand this, what you don't know impacts you to the greatest degree.

**FURTHER STUDY
HOSEA 4:6;
MARK 12:24**

What you hear alone is not enough to make you, except you do something with what you have heard.

FURTHER STUDY
JAMES 1:22

Learn from me: No matter how soft or simple the voice of the Holy Spirit comes to you, don't neglect or trivialize it.

FURTHER STUDY
1 KINGS 19:11-12

The most powerful resource you should possess in life is not money but the word of God.

**FURTHER STUDY
1 TIMOTHY 6:10;
HEBREW 4:12;
EPHESIANS 6:17**

You are the one with the final say, in determining, what happens to you and in your life.

FURTHER STUDY
ROMANS 10:9-10;
MARK 11:23

You release yourself into your purpose through prophetic utterances by your mouth.

**FURTHER STUDY
EZEKIEL 37:3-4;
1 CORINTHIANS 14:39;
PROVERBS 13:3;
JAMES 3:2;
1 PETER 3:2**

Growing unto maturity in God is not a choice but can be a choice if you want to live a life of struggling, even though you are born again.

FURTHER STUDY
GALATIANS 4:1-3;
HEBREW 5:12;
PROVERBS 22:3

The longer you stay away from church (gathering of saints) you cause yourself to wither and faint.

FURTHER STUDY
PROVERBS 15:24, 27:17;
LUKE 22:32;
GALATIANS 5:18;
COLOSSIANS 2:21-22

Your flesh is different from your body. So take care of the body, otherwise; God can't do much through you.

FURTHER STUDY
GALATIANS 5:19-21;
ROMANS 8:3-5;
1 CORINTHIANS 6:19-20

Power and privileges are given to people with proven understanding of responsibilities.

FURTHER STUDY
ACTS 13:2-11;
NEHEMIAH 2:1-8

God does not make people fall in love; don't pray that prayer.

FURTHER STUDY
MATTHEW 24:12, 38-39;
2 TIMOTHY 3: 1-5 (4)

Some opportunities are traps. Live your daily life with discernment through submission to the word of God.

**FURTHER STUDY
HEBREW 5:14;
PHILIPPIANS 4:6;
PSALM 111:130;
HABAKKUK 2:2**

Despondence with life affairs is the direct result of poor or non-existent fellowship with the Holy Spirit.

FURTHER STUDY
EPHESIANS 5: 18-19;
ROMANS 8:26-27; 14:17

If you let the word of God dwell in you richly, of a certainty you loose the opportunity and right to struggle at all for anything.

**FURTHER STUDY
PROVERBS 23:4;
COLOSSIANS 3:16**

The word of God has presence, character, rhythm, and personality.

FURTHER STUDY
JOHN 1:14;
ACT 19:20, 12:24, 20:32

When you walk with God you appear foolish, weak and naïve: You have to accept it and move on to the real deal.

FURTHER STUDY
2 Co 12:9;
1 Corinthians 2:14, 4:10-14

For a person to hold onto, takes pride in the 'I have not mentality', is pathetic, sad and love of tradition.

FURTHER STUDY
MARK 7:13, 12:43-44;
MATTHEW 25:29

The money you don't have at hand or in an account, is not your financial situation.

FURTHER STUDY
2 Co 4:18

You have heard before: experience is the best teacher, but now, i say to you; it is most dangerous to wait for a mistake through experience in order to learn from it.

**FURTHER STUDY
PROVERBS 21:11;
22:3,
27:12**

Do not profane or undermine God's dream that has been imparted to your spirit.

**FURTHER STUDY
HEBREWS 12:16;
1 PETER 2:9;
JEREMIAH 29:11;
1 TIMOTHY 4:14**

When you invest in the continuous expansion of God's ministry for your life, you will never run out of fashion.

FURTHER STUDY
2 CORINTHIANS 3:18

Please, don't mistake persecution for temptation. The former is towards greater degree of glory, whilst the later is the desire of your flesh.

FURTHER STUDY
JAMES 1:13-15

Unforgiveness is too much luxury for a child of God: It's a pollutant to your spirit; producing pain, sickness, strife and instability.

**FURTHER STUDY
LUKE 17:3-4;
MATTHEW 18:21**

Your life is governed by your words. Use it more!

FURTHER STUDY
PSALM 34:12-13;
PROVERBS 6:2

The first place of change is in your mind.

FURTHER STUDY
ROMANS 12:2

What makes a child of God different is that he/she is able to distinguish the truth from the fact.

FURTHER STUDY
2 Co 4:18

You do not enjoy the blessing until you become wholly spirit minded.

FURTHER STUDY
LUKE 9:23;
JOHN 12:26

No matter what you see in front of you, you have the dynamic ability to change it.

FURTHER STUDY
2 CORINTHIANS 4:18;
ACTS 1:8

Heaven is not moved by hearers, but only by doers.

**FURTHER STUDY
REVELATIONS 3:16;
HEBREWS 11:6;
2 CORINTHIANS 9:7;
JAMES 1:22;
2 CORINTHIANS 9:7**

God does not speak Greek and Hebrew language or King James English: He speaks and we hear in any language or ethnic dialect we understand.

**FURTHER STUDY
JOHN 3:12;
ACTS 2:6-11;
GENESIS 11:6-9**

The greatest problem many have is the inability to live by and execute vision.

FURTHER STUDY
JOEL 2:28;
ROMANS 4:20

When you walk with God, you discover time is no longer a force but a factor.

FURTHER STUDY
DANIEL 2:21

There are communications in the spirit realm (dimension of God) that can alter the structure of occurrence, systems and terrestrial protocol, as we 'know' it now.

FURTHER STUDY
2 CORINTHIANS 12:4

The mustard seed [first level] faith is the recognition of God and your rights in Christ. In other words, if you believe in God and Jesus Christ, you have Faith. Howbeit this level of faith is not enough to extinguish the different types of fiery arrows the enemies throws at you.

FURTHER STUDY
JOHN 17:2-3;
HEBREWS 11: 6;
1 CORINTHIANS 3:21

Your aspirations for growth and depth in God, determines the kind of message (teaching and preaching) you listen to (desire).

**FURTHER STUDY
MATTHEW 28: 19-20;
JOHN 6:53-56, 66-68;
GALATIANS 3:1;
1 TIMOTHY 4:6;
MATTHEW 6:33-34**

Many people are entering the future without effective Spirit-filled preparation. This is sure guaranty for instability and disappointment.

**FURTHER STUDY
EPHESIANS 5:18;
PROVERBS 4:1-10,
22:6**

There are things God cannot tell you until you grow into spiritual maturity.

FURTHER STUDY
1 CORINTHIANS 3:1-3;
JOHN 16:12, 3:12

Many people are not happy and successful because they lack fellowship with the Holy Spirit.

**FURTHER STUDY
JOSHUA 1:8;
PSALM 1:1-3;
JAMES 4:3;
JOHN 14: 16-18**

When you start walking with God, you discover his formula is different: spiritual versus scientific, illogical versus logic, truth versus fact.

FURTHER STUDY
2 KINGS 6:5-7;
NUMBERS 20:7-8;
2 CHRONICLES 20:21-24;
LUKE 5:4-5;
ACTS 8:39-40, 28: 4-6

People, who give attention to observe humanity's and nature's design by God including understanding the patterns and laws that governs the terrestrial and universe, live a life above limitations.

FURTHER STUDY
MATTHEW 18:19;
ECCLESIASTES 3:1-2;
GENESIS 1: 14, 8:22

Until you come into unity in the spirit there is just so much you can do.

FURTHER STUDY
JOHN 17:21;
ACTS 2:1-2, 5:12;
2 CHRONICLES 5:13-14

God's Spirit is He who transforms, regenerates, revitalizes and reveals.

FURTHER STUDY
ZECHARIAH 4:6;
ROMANS 8:11

If you walk with God, living is not at random or a probability: no circumstances will take you by surprise, not even the natural 'sleep' (death in other words) in old age.

FURTHER STUDY
JEREMIAH 29: 11;
JOHN 16:13;
ACTS 21-23,
27:9-10

What you need to be part of is a ministry not just a church.

FURTHER STUDY
EPHESIANS 4:12;
2 CORINTHIANS 5:18

When God gives you an instruction, train and discipline yourself to see it through at the specified time (doing the right, rightly)

**FURTHER STUDY
1 KINGS 13:1-32;
JUDGES 13:5,
16:16-19**

No one has enough excuse to be unsuccessful, if full of the word of God.

FURTHER STUDY
PHILIPPIANS 2:13, 4:13;
1 TIMOTHY 4:15;
3 JOHN 2

When you study the word long enough you will discover there is something called the speed of the spirit.

FURTHER STUDY
1 KINGS 18:45-46

As the move of God in your life deepens, grows and prevails, favor becomes bread.

FURTHER STUDY
PROVERBS 16:7

The ten primary responsibilities of a true Minister are to: Educate, Inform, Train, Equip, Edify, Inspire, Impart, Lead, Support and Encourage God's people for the work of Ministry.

**FURTHER STUDY
EPHESIANS 4:11-12;
1 TIMOTHY 4:6**

You should be the reason why people come to Christ.

**FURTHER STUDY
MATTHEW 5:16;
1 TIMOTHY 4:12;
EPHESIANS 4:29**

To successfully implement any idea, the value of $1,000 is relative-same to $10,000 for a start up capital.

FURTHER STUDY
MATTHEW 25:24-28

The reason for the barricade in your life is because you gave it an existence.

FURTHER STUDY
2 CORINTHIANS 4:18

The Holy Spirit in your life brings you a competitive edge.

**FURTHER STUDY
JOHN 14:26**

Refuse your senses to relocate you away from God's blessings.

**FURTHER STUDY
2 CORINTHIANS 4:18;
EPHESIANS 1:3**

When you are driven by the vision God gives; the way you plan, organize and spend your money will be different.

FURTHER STUDY
MATTHEW 6:33;
HABAKKUK 2:2

Giving for charity amounts to good deeds, but it is an impact investment when you give your offerings, tithes and first fruits to the house of God and where applicable partnerships.

FURTHER STUDY
PHILIPPIANS 4:17;
2 CORINTHIANS 9:6-8 (AMP);
1 TIMOTHY 5:17 (AMP);

There are prayers we should answer as Christians full of the Spirit: When people ask, where is the light? Be the answer!

FURTHER STUDY
HEBREWS 4:16;
MATTHEW 5:14, 10:8

The word of God from the mouth of a Minister of God, is God talking.

FURTHER STUDY
1 KINGS 17:1;
1 JOHN 4:17;
MATTHEW 16:19, 18:18;
1 THESSALONIANS 2:13

The spirit of Man is created with four faces (sides); which are: his communion with God; his interaction with the spirit realm; his influence with creation; and his fellowship with mankind.

FURTHER STUDY
GENESIS 1:26;
EZEKIEL 1:5-11

The depth of the supernatural you experience is in direct proportion to the degree of the flesh you give up.

FURTHER STUDY
JOHN 12:24

God does not make people fall in love, stop praying that prayer.

**FURTHER STUDY
DEUTERONOMY 30:19;
JAMES 4:3;
GENESIS 12:24**

ABOUT THE AUTHOR

Apostle Emmanuel Etim is a multi-faceted, uniquely different and uncommon minister of the Gospel. At the age of eight, he met with Jesus Christ in the glorified body. By the laying of hands, he was commissioned with power to heal the sick, cast out devils, raise the dead, work miracles, and teach all to observe such as Christ commands. **Perfecting the saints.**

The central theme of his message is the Spirit Life "John 3:6; Gal 5:25; and John 4:23" travelling extensively throughout the world, Apostle Emmanuel Etim teaches, imparts and demonstrates the power of Christ love and bearing witness to the evidence that Jesus was dead but now He is Alive.

President of Emmanuel Etim Ministries, he is also the founder and Snr Pastor of Spirit Life, a non-denominational church headquartered in Lagos, Nigeria with International Office(s) in Addis Ababa, Ethiopia; London, UK and the United States of America.

Follow the author on Fcebook.com/Apostle Emmanuel Etim; Instagram and Twitter @apostleemmaetim

www.ingramcontent.com/pod-product-compliance
Lightning Source LLC
Chambersburg PA
CBHW031408040426
42444CB00005B/464